Fast Facts About Insects & Spiders

Fast Facts About
BEES

by Lisa J. Amstutz

Raintree is an imprint of Capstone Global Library Limited, a company incorporated in England and Wales having its registered office at 264 Banbury Road, Oxford, OX2 7DY – Registered company number: 6695582

www.raintree.co.uk
myorders@raintree.co.uk

Edited by Abby Huff
Designed by Kyle Grenz
Original illustrations © Capstone Global Library Limited 2022
Picture research by Jo Miller
Production by Tori Abraham
Originated by Capstone Global Library Ltd

978 1 3982 1334 0 (hardback)
978 1 3982 1333 3 (paperback)

British Library Cataloguing in Publication Data
A full catalogue record for this book is available from the British Library.

Acknowledgements
We would like to thank the following for permission to reproduce photographs: Dreamstime: Tacio Philip Sansonovski, 5; Science Source: Scott Camazine, 18; Shutterstock: BlueRingMedia, 9, Christian Musat, 14, Debbie Steinhausser, 13, Dionisvera, cover, Fevziie, 15, HLD1, 21, Inspiration GP, 20 (left), Ivan Marjanovic, 11, Ikordela, 16, Noble Nature, 17, Ruth Swan, 7, StGrafix, 6, Vitaly Zorkin, 20 (right), WitthayaP, 20 (middle), Young Swee Ming, 19, Yuttana Joe, 10, zabavina (background), cover and throughout

Every effort has been made to contact copyright holders of material reproduced in this book. Any omissions will be rectified in subsequent printings if notice is given to the publisher.

All the internet addresses (URLs) given in this book were valid at the time of going to press. However, due to the dynamic nature of the internet, some addresses may have changed, or sites may have changed or ceased to exist since publication. While the author and publisher regret any inconvenience this may cause readers, no responsibility for any such changes can be accepted by either the author or the publisher.

Contents

Words in **bold** are in the glossary.

All about bees

Bees are flying **insects**. They have two sets of wings. They make a buzzing noise when they fly.

Bees have three body sections. They also have two **antennae** and six legs. Female bees have a stinger. They use it to protect themselves. A bee's sting is painful.

antennae

wings

legs

stinger

Bees live all around the world. But not in Antarctica! It is too cold there. Some bees live in holes. They make holes in soil or wood. Others make big nests called **hives**.

There are more than 20,000 types of bees. Some have black and yellow stripes. Others are red, blue, green or black.

A bee's life

A female bee lays eggs. Soon a tiny **larva** wriggles out of each egg. It eats honey. It also eats a powder from flowers called pollen. It gets bigger and bigger.

Next, the insect forms a **pupa**. Its body changes inside this shell. Finally, an adult bee comes out. The bee flies away.

Bee life cycle

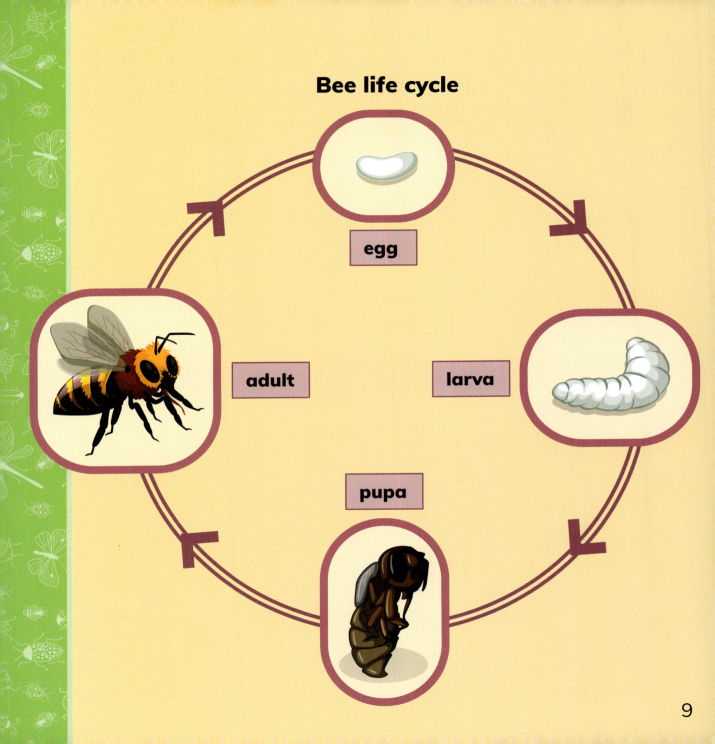

egg

larva

pupa

adult

Inside the nest

Some types of bees live alone. A female makes a nest. She lays eggs inside it. She leaves food for her young to eat. Then she flies away.

A leafcutter bee makes her nest with leaves.

Honeybees live in large groups. Each bee has a job. The queen lays eggs. Males **mate** with the queen. Female worker bees gather food. They also guard the nest.

workers

queen

Honeybees live in hives. This nest is made from wax. Bees make the wax in their bodies. Then they chew the wax. They shape it into rooms with six sides.

Each room is called a **cell**. Many cells make up the hive. Some cells hold food. The queen lays eggs in others.

cell

Feeding and flowers

Bees fly from flower to flower to get food. They eat two things from flowers. One is a sweet liquid called **nectar**. The other is powdery pollen.

Bees eat honey too. They make this food.
Honeybees spit nectar into cells in the hive.
They flap their wings. This dries the nectar.
Soon it thickens into honey.

We need bees! Bees **pollinate** plants. Pollen from a flower sticks to a bee's body. It rubs off on the next flower. This helps fruits and seeds grow.

pollen

Beekeepers raise honeybees. They
gather honey for people to eat. Do you like
eating honey? Then you can thank a bee!

Fun facts

- When a honeybee finds food, it does a dance. The dance shows the other bees where to go.

- Each honeybee hive has only one queen. She can lay up to 2,000 eggs per day!

A honeybee (middle) does the waggle dance.

sweat bee

- Sweat bees like to drink human sweat! Don't worry, though. These tiny bees don't often sting.

- Carpenter bees make nests in wood. They sometimes make holes in wooden buildings.

Draw a honeybee hive

What you need:

- paper
- pencil
- felt-tips or crayons

What to do:

1. Draw a picture of a hive. Add lots of six-sided cells.

2. Draw some eggs and honey in the cells.

3. Now add bees to your hive!

Glossary

antenna feeler on an insect's head used to touch and smell

cell six-sided room made from wax inside a hive; bees store pollen, nectar, honey and eggs in cells

hive nest where a group of bees live

insect small animal with a hard outer shell, six legs, three body sections and two antennae

larva insect at the stage of its life cycle between an egg and a pupa

mate join with another to produce young

nectar sweet liquid found in many flowers

pollinate move pollen from flower to flower; pollinating helps flowers make seeds

pupa insect at the stage of its life cycle between a larva and an adult

Find out more

Books

Bees and Wasps: Secrets of Their Busy Colonies (Amazing Animal Colonies), Sara L. Latta (Raintree, 2019)

Bees and Wasps, James Maclaine (Usborne, 2013)

Insects and Spiders: Explore Nature with Fun Facts and Activities (Nature Explorers), DK (DK Children, 2019)

Websites

www.bbc.com/bitesize/articles/zx4ktv4
Learn more about why bees are attracted to flowers.

www.dkfindout.com/uk/animals-and-nature/insects/bee-colonies
Find out more about bee colonies.

Index